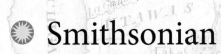
Smithsonian

Exploring
the
New York
Colony

D1716487

by Patrick Catel

CAPSTONE PRESS
a capstone imprint

Smithsonian books are published by Capstone Press,
1710 Roe Crest Drive, North Mankato, Minnesota 56003
www.capstonepub.com

Library of Congress Cataloging-in-Publication Data
Names: Catel, Patrick, author.
Title: Exploring the New York Colony/by Patrick Catel.
Description: North Mankato, Minnesota: Smithsonian Books, an imprint of Capstone Press, 2017
Series: Smithsonian. Exploring the 13 Colonies | Includes bibliographical references and index.
Audience: Grades 4–6.
Identifiers: LCCN 2016006115
ISBN 9781515722342 (library binding)
ISBN 9781515722472 (paperback)
ISBN 9781515722601 (ebook PDF)
Subjects: LCSH: New York (State)—History—Colonial period, ca. 1600–1775—Juvenile literature. New York
(State)—History—Revolution, 1775–1783—Juvenile literature. New York (N.Y.)—History—Colonial period,
ca. 1600–1775—Juvenile literature. New York (N.Y.)—History—Revolution, 1775–1783—Juvenile literature.
Classification: LCC F128.4 .C38 2017 | DDC 974.7/02—dc23
LC record available at http://lccn.loc.gov/2016006115

Editorial Credits
Jennifer Huston, editor; Richard Parker, designer; Eric Gohl, media researcher;
Kathy McColley, production specialist

Our very special thanks to Stephen Binns at the Smithsonian Center for Learning and Digital Access for
his curatorial review. Capstone would also like to thank Kealy Gordon, Smithsonian Institution Product
Development Manager, and the following at Smithsonian Enterprises: Christopher A. Liedel, President;
Carol LeBlanc, Senior Vice President; Brigid Ferraro, Vice President; Ellen Nanney, Licensing Manager.

Printed and bound in the USA.
009669F16

Table of Contents

Introduction:
The 13 Colonies

In the early 1600s, many people looking for a better life left their homes in Europe to establish colonies in North America. A colony is a place settled by people from another country. Although they've moved to the colony, they are still subject to the laws of their original homeland. During the next 100 years or so, 13 English colonies were established along the eastern coast of North America.

The English weren't the first people to make their homes in North America. In fact they weren't even the first Europeans to explore the continent. But these 13 Colonies would eventually become the United States of America.

People from the Netherlands, who are known as the Dutch, settled in the New York Colony before the English.

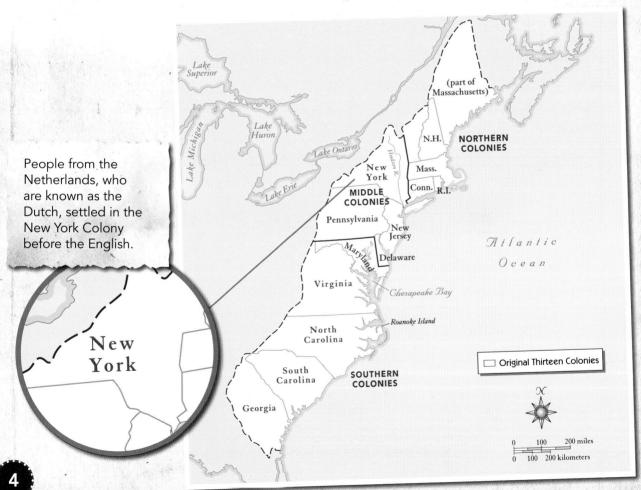

While sailing west across the Atlantic Ocean from Spain in 1492, Christopher Columbus (pictured here) found North America, a continent unknown to Europeans at the time.

The "New World"

In the early 1500s, North America was the "New World." Europeans had only recently discovered that it existed. Adventurers from Spain, France, England, and the Netherlands all sailed across the Atlantic to the New World. Some came in search of gold or other riches. Others were looking for a shortcut to Asia. They brought back fascinating tales of a rich land full of **natural resources**. It wasn't long before people began moving there.

natural resource—something in nature that people use, such as coal and trees

Colonial Characteristics

In 1513 explorer Juan Ponce de León arrived in what is now Florida and quickly claimed the land for Spain. In 1565 the Spanish established a settlement there called St. Augustine. This was the first permanent European settlement in what became the United States.

The first permanent English settlement in North America was established in Virginia in 1607. Other settlements and colonies soon developed as more Europeans decided to make the New World their home.

Each of the 13 Colonies had its own special characteristics. These differences stemmed from who first settled there and why. Some hoped to get rich off the land. Others came to worship freely. In many places in Europe, certain religions were not allowed or were looked down upon. The Maryland Colony was a safe place for Catholics to practice their faith. Quakers started the colony of Pennsylvania.

Juan Ponce de León

Regardless of their reasons, the settlers came to stay. But it wasn't easy starting a new life in a new land. Beginning with the long ocean voyage, the colonists faced hunger, disease, and even death. But they risked it all on the hope of creating a better life for themselves and their families.

Few women were among the first settlers in Colonial America. After around 1620, their numbers increased.

The Original 13 Colonies
The first permanent European settlement in each colony:

Virginia	1607	Delaware	1638
Massachusetts	1620	Pennsylvania	1643
New Hampshire	1623	North Carolina	1653
New York	1624	New Jersey	1660
Connecticut	1633	South Carolina	1670
Maryland	1634	Georgia	1733
Rhode Island	1636		

Chapter 1:
Native Peoples of New York

When Europeans arrived two major groups of Native Americans were already living in the New York region: the Algonquian and Iroquois. The Mohicans, Lenni Lenapes, and Montauks were part of the Algonquian group. The Lenni Lenapes and Montauks lived near the Atlantic coast. The Mohicans lived in the Hudson River Valley. The Mohawks, Oneidas, Onondagas, Cayugas, and Senecas made up the Iroquois group. They lived further inland.

In the 1500s Manhattan Island was home to Native Americans who lived in longhouses.

Colonist John White painted this scene to show what an Algonquian village looked like.

The Algonquian People

Algonquian men were expert hunters and fishermen. **Shellfish** from rivers and coastal waters were a large part of the Algonquian diet. Women did most of the farm work, growing crops such as corn, beans, and squash. The Algonquian people also gathered leaves, seeds, berries, roots, and nuts. They even made maple syrup.

The Algonquians lived in homes called wigwams. Wigwams were made using wooden poles tied together to form a dome-shaped frame. The frame was then covered with long grasses, reeds, or bark. A fire inside the wigwam was used for cooking and warmth. Each wigwam usually housed two or three **generations** of a single family.

The Iroquois People

The Iroquois people also hunted, fished, and farmed. But because they lived farther away from the sea, they relied more on farming. Their villages were often larger than Algonquian villages, usually with a few hundred people. To protect themselves from other tribes, the Iroquois built defensive walls around their villages and crops.

The Iroquois people lived in long, narrow cabins called longhouses. These were made from poles shaped into an arched roof and covered with sheets of bark. Longhouses were between 40 and 400 feet long, depending on how many families lived in each house. Each longhouse had interior walls to divide the building into compartments. Usually a single family lived in each compartment.

shellfish—a sea animal protected by a shell; clams, oysters, and crabs are shellfish

generation—a group of people born around the same time

Trade and Trouble

When the settlers first arrived, the Native Americans taught them how to plant and harvest a variety of fruits and vegetables. The native people also knew which plants could be used as medicines and which were poisonous. Without the help of Native Americans, the first European settlers likely would not have survived.

For many years the tribes and the colonists traded peacefully with each other. The Native Americans wanted guns, metal tools, glass beads, fabrics, and other items. The colonists were happy to trade these items for food, land, and lumber. They also traded for animal furs that they could sell in Europe for a lot of money.

The Native Americans were skilled at growing corn and other crops. They taught the first settlers how to grow these crops, which helped the newcomers to survive.

Decline of the Native Americans

The Europeans also brought with them diseases, such as **smallpox**, that the Native Americans had never been exposed to. Many of them died because their bodies could not fight the foreign germs.

The Dutch were the first European settlers in present-day New York. They were happy to trade with the Native Americans for food and furs.

In addition, as more Europeans arrived and the colonies grew, many Native Americans were forced from their land. They were not happy that the colonists were taking their land and hunting grounds. This often led to violence. By the 1700s disease and several years of conflicts with the settlers had nearly wiped out the Algonquian people.

smallpox—a disease that spreads easily from person to person, causing chills, fever, and pimples that scar

Chapter 2:
New Netherland

Historians believe that in 1524 Italian explorer Giovanni da Verrazzano was the first European to see New York Harbor. In 1609 French explorer Samuel de Champlain may have been the first European to set foot in what is now New York.

That same year the Dutch East India Company, a trading company, sent English explorer Henry Hudson to North America. The Dutch were hoping he could find a faster way to the Pacific Ocean and Asia. When Hudson and his crew arrived in the New World, they sailed up a river that was later named after him. They got as far as present-day Albany before realizing that the river was not going to lead them to the Pacific. Even so, Hudson claimed the surrounding lands for the Dutch.

In 1609 Henry Hudson's ship, the *Half Moon*, arrived at the river that would later bear his name.

Henry Hudson (1565?–1611?)

He only made four voyages in his lifetime, but Henry Hudson is one of the most famous explorers in history. Each time he set sail, Hudson was looking for a shorter, more direct route to the Pacific Ocean and Asia. Although he never found what he was seeking, Hudson made several discoveries in North America and inspired others to explore there as well.

The details surrounding Hudson's death are a mystery. In June 1611, after exploring a large bay between present-day Quebec and Ontario, Canada, Hudson and his crew headed home. But many of Hudson's men were angry and fed up with him. Some of them led a **mutiny** and seized control of the ship. The crew sailed away, leaving Hudson, his son, and seven others in a small boat to survive on their own. They were never seen again. Historians believe they died on the large bay in Canada that we now know as Hudson Bay.

Founding of New Netherland

After his trip, Hudson raved about the natural beauty of the region. His descriptions of the plentiful wildlife attracted Dutch fur traders, who built Fort Nassau, a trading post in present-day Albany.

> *"The land is the finest for cultivation that I ever in my life set foot upon, and it also abounds in trees of every description."*
>
> —Henry Hudson's description of the land that would become New York

In 1614 the New Netherland Company was created for fur trading in North America. But it took 10 years before the first settlers **colonized** New Netherland, which included parts of present-day New York, New Jersey, Delaware, Connecticut, and Pennsylvania. At first few people wanted to move there. Jobs were plentiful in the Netherlands, so people were not willing to risk their lives traveling to the new colony.

But in the spring of 1624, a group of about 30 families arrived in New Netherland. Some of them built Fort Orange, a fur-trading post near the site of Fort Nassau, which had been destroyed. In 1626 additional colonists started a settlement on Manhattan Island. They named the settlement New Amsterdam after the capital city of the Netherlands. These were the first permanent European settlements in what is now New York.

Settlers got to work building a settlement on Manhattan Island, home to what is now New York City.

mutiny—a revolt against the captain of a ship
colonize—to formally settle a new territory

Critical Thinking with Primary Sources

In 1626, Peter Minuit, the governor of New Netherland, made a deal with the Lenni Lenape tribe. In exchange for goods such as tools, cloth, and other household items, Minuit obtained Manhattan Island. In the letter shown here, Peter Schaghen, a representative of the Dutch East and West India Companies, recorded the purchase. It says they purchased Manhattan for 60 guilders. In 1846 a historian calculated that sum to be around $24. That would be less than $700 today. Why do you think the Lenni Lenapes sold the land? Do you think they knew they were selling all of their rights to Manhattan Island? Was it a fair deal?

The Land

In New Netherland the Dutch found a land with mountains and plains divided by major rivers. Land was plentiful and much of it was suitable for farming. The vast forests were abundant with wildlife. This was quite different from Europe. There people lived more closely together, and resources were more scarce. To the European newcomers, America seemed like an untouched land of endless beauty and natural resources.

In the mid-1620s, New Amsterdam (now called New York City) was a small but growing settlement.

A Variety of Cultures

Within a year New Netherland was home to about 250 Dutch settlers. The Netherlands welcomed people of different countries and religions, so New Netherland did the same. But the Dutch West India Company held a **monopoly** on the fur-trading industry. This meant that all fur traders living in New Netherland had to work for the Dutch West India Company. However, they could make more money as independent fur traders. Because of this restriction, New Netherland grew at a much slower pace than the English colonies in North America. By the 1640s there were only about 500 settlers in New Netherland. In comparison some of the English colonies had 40,000 to 50,000 residents.

New Amsterdam

New York City—now home to nearly 8.5 million people—began in April 1625 as a Dutch trading post called New Amsterdam. It took a lot of hard work just to make the settlement suitable for living. Trees had to be cut down to build homes and plant crops. Within a few years, New Amsterdam was a small but growing town. There was even a wall around the city to protect the settlers from pirates and Native American attacks.

Did You Know?

An area close to the wall surrounding New Amsterdam became known as Wall Street. Although the wall itself no longer exists, the name lives on. It's now home to the New York Stock Exchange and is the heart of America's financial center.

monopoly—a situation in which there is only one supplier of a good or service, and therefore that supplier can control the price

New Leadership

By the late 1630s, New Amsterdam was neglected and falling into disrepair. Farms were overgrown and homes and buildings were falling apart. Crime was also on the rise. When Willem Kieft took over as governor of New Netherland in 1638, he put strict new laws in place. During his reign the Dutch West India Company gave up its monopoly on the fur trade. The company believed it could make more money by collecting taxes from fur traders instead. Once the monopoly was lifted, new settlers arrived from Virginia, Maryland, and Massachusetts.

From the start, Kieft was very unpopular as governor. Just a year after he took the position, he made a mistake that would cost thousands of lives.

A Deadly Mistake

In 1639 Kieft tried to force the Lenni Lenapes to pay taxes in the form of corn or wampum, beads used by Native Americans as money. Kieft reasoned that the taxes were to protect the Native Americans from attacks by the fierce Mohawk tribe. This made the Lenni Lenapes very angry. They had been friendly and generous to the European settlers, giving them food and helping them survive in the wilderness. They didn't need protection from the Mohawks. If anything *they* protected the settlers from attacks.

In October 1643 Native Americans set fire to several homes at the Pavonia settlement. Many settlers died. Those who survived fled to New Amsterdam.

The Dutch and Native Americans signed a peace treaty at Fort Amsterdam.

When the Lenni Lenapes refused to pay the taxes, Kieft ordered raids on their villages. The Native Americans fought back, setting the stage for four years of fighting with the settlers.

The Pig War

In the summer of 1640, some property on Staten Island was destroyed and several pigs were stolen. Kieft accused the Lenni Lenape tribe of the crime and sent a group of 100 men to get the pigs back. But things quickly turned violent when Kieft's men tortured and killed several of the Native Americans, who claimed they were innocent. And they were. It was later revealed that sailors working for the Dutch West India Company likely stole the pigs.

The Lenni Lenapes sought revenge the following year. They burned the settlement on Staten Island and killed many of its residents. By 1642 more than 1,000 settlers and Native Americans had been killed in battles. In April of that year, Jonas Bronck, an **immigrant** from Sweden, helped negotiate peace between Kieft and the Native Americans. The site of Bronck's large farm is now the Bronx, one of New York City's five **boroughs**.

immigrant—a person who moves from one country to live permanently in another

borough—one of the five divisions of New York City: Brooklyn, the Bronx, Manhattan, Queens, and Staten Island

Out with the Old, In with the New

All the violence and bloodshed had erased many of the things Kieft had done to improve the colony. When Kieft decided to tax the colonists to pay for reconstruction, they were furious. It wasn't long before Kieft was fired as governor.

His replacement was military hero Peter Stuyvesant. As much as Kieft had tried to improve the colony, when Stuyvesant arrived in May 1647, the place was still a shambles. In New Amsterdam, buildings were falling down and garbage littered the streets.

Stuyvesant quickly set strict new laws. He also organized a police patrol and a "bucket brigade" to fight fires. He paved streets and made efforts to improve education. But in order to pay for these improvements, Stuyvesant placed taxes on furs, wine, and liquor.

THE WALL.

Peter Stuyvesant (third from right) discusses improvements to be made to New Amsterdam. The men stand before the wall that surrounded the city.

The colonists weren't happy with the additional taxes. Even so, Stuyvesant served as governor for 17 years. During that time he cleaned up New Amsterdam by creating a garbage dump and setting up building codes and traffic regulations. The colony's population also increased from 2,000 to nearly 9,000 during his time in office.

During his time as governor, Peter Stuyvesant made many improvements to New Amsterdam, such as paving the streets.

Peter Stuyvesant (1592?–1672)

Born in the Netherlands, Peter Stuyvesant worked for the Dutch West India Company. In 1644 he lost a leg during a battle with the Spanish in the Caribbean. As the governor of New Netherland, Stuyvesant strengthened Dutch power in the region. However, he did not like giving other people a say in the government. His stubbornness and gruff manner made him many enemies.

Chapter 3:
Becoming New York

England and the Netherlands had been **allies** in the past. However, by the mid-1600s the two countries were competing for goods and land in America. The English wanted New Netherland because it was located between their New England and Maryland colonies. England's King Charles II gave his brother James, the Duke of York, land in America that included New Netherland. But first the English had to take the land from the Dutch.

New Netherland prospered under the control of Peter Stuyvesant, but he was an unpopular leader. In late August 1664, a fleet of English warships carrying more than 400 troops sailed into what is now New York Harbor. They were ready to go to battle with the Dutch to take over New Amsterdam.

James, the Duke of York

Stuyvesant tried to rally troops, but the Dutch settlers offered him no support. Instead they drew up a document outlining the terms of their surrender. With no military support to back him up, Stuyvesant was forced to surrender New Amsterdam to the English. Without firing a single shot, the British took control of the city. Soon after they took over all of New Netherland.

ally—a person or country that helps and supports another

In 1664 the Peter Stuyvesant surrenders New Netherland to the English without a fight.

Critical Thinking with Primary Sources

The Dutch wrote up their own terms of surrender to the English. In the document shown here, which point talks about the Dutch being allowed to keep their land? Which point talks about freedom of religion?

3. All people shall continue [to] enjoy their Lands, Houses, Goods, Ships ...

6. It is consented to, that any people may freely come from the Netherlands and plant in this Country ...

8. The Dutch here shall enjoy their Liberty of ... Divine Worship and Church Dissipline.

9. No Dutchman here or Dutch ship here shall upon any occasion be prest to serve in Warr against any Nation whatsoever.

The Founding of New York

With the English in control, New Netherland became the New York Colony and New Amsterdam became New York City. The English allowed the Dutch people living there to keep their property and freedom of religion. They were also given more say in the government.

In August 1673, after a brief war, the Dutch recaptured New York. But when the two countries signed a peace treaty the following year, the British regained control of the colony.

After the English took control of New Netherland, the Dutch were able to continue living there and keep their customs.

After he was removed from power, King James II (lower right in blue coat) fled to France.

Governing New York

New York's residents always wanted more say in the government. In 1683 the Duke of York gave them more freedom to govern themselves. Among other things they were given the right to impose taxes and create laws. They also elected 17 representatives to New York's first General Assembly. The representatives wrote the Charter of Liberties and Privileges, which granted freedom of religion to New York's Christian residents. It also gave all male landowners the right to vote.

Changes in Power

When King Charles II died in February 1685, his brother James, the Duke of York, became king. King James II soon took away the liberties he'd given the colonists. He shut down the New York Assembly and made the colony part of the government of New England. This made the colonists very unhappy. King James wasn't popular in England either. When a rebellion broke out in England in 1688, he was forced from power.

Chapter 4:
Daily Life in Colonial New York

Life in the 13 Colonies was hard work. Many people in cities such as New York City were involved in the fur trade or other trade across the Atlantic. Clothes makers, blacksmiths, bakers, and other craftsmen lived and worked in cities.

Outside the city most settlers lived off the land, growing crops or hunting for all of their food. The father of a family usually ran the family farm or a business. Farmers grew corn, beans, squash, wheat, oats, and barley. Colonial families had to cut down trees to clear land in order to plant crops. Then they used the logs to build their homes.

Children also pitched in and helped on the farm and in the home. They milked cows and collected eggs from the family's chickens. Boys chopped wood, while girls collected water from a well or nearby stream.

Critical Thinking with Primary Sources

There weren't many schools in Colonial times, so children were often taught in teachers' homes. These were called "dame schools." Compare this painting of a dame school in Colonial times to your classroom. How is it similar? How is it different?

School Life

Education was very important to the Dutch colonists of New Netherland. They believed that both boys and girls should get an education. But in the English colonies, only boys went to school.

Children were taught reading, spelling, grammar, and arithmetic. They also studied the Bible. New Amsterdam had its first school by 1638. But after the British took over, public education in New York lagged behind many of the other colonies. Wealthy parents hired tutors. Others taught their children to read and write at home. Some went to religious schools, but many had no schooling at all.

Women's Rights

The wife's main role was always raising children and taking care of the home. But women had more rights when the colony was under Dutch rule. Unlike married women in the British colonies, women in New Netherland could own property and run businesses. Rather than taking their husband's last name, they also kept their maiden names when they got married.

Women had more rights when New York was under Dutch rule. The woman in black (third from right with arm raised) was a Quaker preacher.

Slavery in New Netherland

The Dutch West India Company allowed slavery in New Netherland. The slaves were captured Africans forced to work in America without pay. Many people died on the brutal, crowded journey across the Atlantic Ocean from Africa. Some slaves were forever torn apart from their families.

The first slaves arrived in New Netherland in 1626. However, slavery was not as common there as it was in some of the British colonies of North America. In the 1640s the Dutch put a system into place called half-freedom. Under this system some slaves were granted partial freedom. They were given their own farms and were allowed to sell their crops. However, they were required to pay an annual tax and perform labor for the Dutch West India Company when needed.

When slaves arrived in America, they were sold to the highest bidder. This painting shows a slave auction in New Amsterdam in 1655.

Slavery in Colonial New York

Once the British took over in 1664, slavery became more common in New York. It is estimated that 41 percent of all households in New York City had slaves during the Colonial period. Only Charles Town, South Carolina, had more slaves.

Slaves in the Southern Colonies labored mainly on farms and plantations. But most slaves in New York worked in homes or businesses. Women and some men worked in homes as servants. Other male slaves were taught a trade or craft, such as carpentry or **silversmithing**. Slaves also performed much of the heavy labor that helped the colony survive. They cut down trees, cleared land for planting, and built roads, hospitals, and churches.

Slaves who worked as servants, maids, or cooks inside homes had much better lives than those who labored in fields.

Slaves were treated more harshly when the British took over. The British got rid of the half-freedom system. They also passed strict new laws forbidding slaves from owning property and gathering in groups.

After the Revolutionary War, many people began to think that slavery went against the freedom Americans had fought for. Over time the state of New York even became a center for the **abolitionist** movement. By 1820 about 95 percent of all African-Americans living in New York City were free. By 1827 nearly all blacks in the state were free.

silversmith—a person who makes items out of silver
abolitionist—a person who worked to end slavery

Chapter 5:
Becoming a British Colony

Over the years the New York Colony continued to grow. When the British took over in 1664, the population was around 9,000. The colony's population grew rapidly during the next century. In 1771 there were 168,000 residents. That number more than doubled over the next 20 years. In 1790 there were over 340,000 people living in New York.

At first few people settled on the land west and north of Albany. The settlers feared attacks from Native Americans and from the French to the north, in present-day Canada. The French and English were longtime enemies, and fighting often broke out in Europe and America. Between 1689 and 1763, the English and the French went to war four times in Colonial America. The fighting was mainly for control of land in North America and the valuable fur trade.

New York City: A Melting Pot of Cultures

The Dutch had encouraged people from a variety of countries and cultures to settle in New Netherland. This practice remained the same when the British took over. The promise of religious freedom drew Catholics, Jews, and Protestant groups, such as Baptists and French Huguenots, to New York. Immigrants arrived from Germany, France, Scotland, and Ireland. This mixture of ethnic and religious groups helped New York become the melting pot of diverse cultures that it still is today.

Conflicts Between France and England

King William's War 1689–1697

Queen Anne's War 1702–1713

King George's War 1744–1748

French and Indian War 1754–1763

The British clash with the French and their Native American allies during the French and Indian War.

New York City thrived under British rule. When the city came under British control, there were about 1,500 people living there. By 1790 the city was home to 33,000 residents.

New York City soon became a major shipping port and a center of trade. As the city grew, it attracted merchants and a variety of business professionals, including bankers and lawyers. At the same time, the city was still home to many farms. It was not uncommon for livestock to be seen roaming the city streets.

Adopting British Customs

The Dutch were allowed to keep many of their customs and traditions when the British took control. But as more people moved to New York from England, the colony adopted many British customs, although this didn't happen overnight. As one colonist complained in a letter from May 1692, "Our chiefest unhappyness here is too great a mixture of nations and English [the] least part."

Over time, as Dutch–style buildings became rundown, new ones were built in the English style. Wealthy New Yorkers also started dressing like their rich counterparts in London. Powdered wigs were popular with both men and women of the upper class.

Even as New York City grew, Manhattan Island was still home to many farms in the late 1600s.

By the late 1700s, most of the farms were gone and New York City was a thriving center of business and trade.

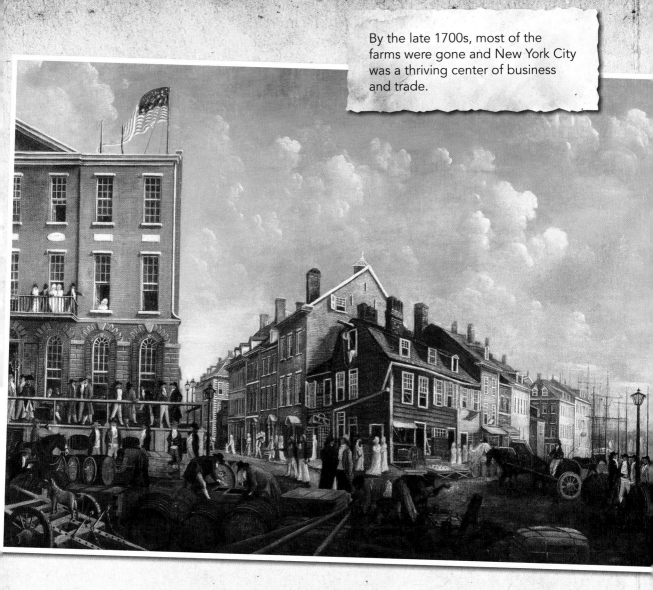

"In size it comes next to Boston and Philadelphia, but with regard to fine buildings, opulence, and extensive commerce, it vies with them for supremacy ... I found it extremely pleasant to walk in the town, for it seemed like a garden."

—Swedish-Finnish explorer Peter Kalm's description of New York City in 1750

Chapter 6:
The Road to War

By 1750 about 80,000 people lived in the New York Colony. After its defeat in the French and Indian War, France gave up much of its territory in North America. New France became another British colony called Canada. With the threat of the French gone, New York and the other 12 colonies grew even faster. By 1775 New York's population was an estimated 190,000.

Costs of the French and Indian War

Although Great Britain no longer had to worry about France in North America, its troubles were far from over. The war cost a lot of money. Great Britain also sent troops to protect colonists and guard the frontier, which was expensive.

After the French and Indian War, Britain's King George III issued the Proclamation of 1763. The proclamation made it illegal for colonists to settle west of the Appalachian Mountains. The land shown in pink on the map was set aside for Native Americans.

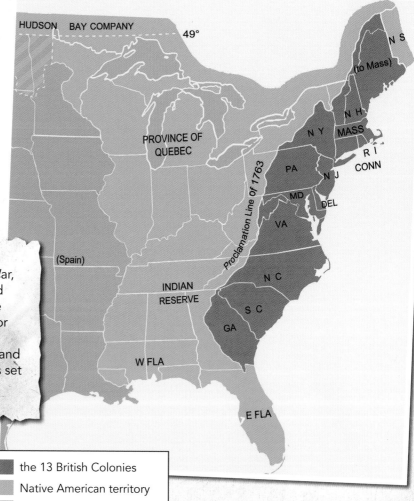

the 13 British Colonies

Native American territory

Spanish territory

Tax Hikes = Angry Colonists

British authorities thought that the colonists should help pay for the war and their protection. As a result they ordered the colonists to pay new taxes. The first major new tax was the Sugar Act of 1764. The Sugar Act taxed certain goods coming into and out of the colonies, such as sugar and coffee. In October 1764 the New York Assembly protested the Sugar Act, saying the taxes would hurt local businesses.

On November 1, 1765, the British **Parliament** passed the Stamp Act. This put a tax on all paper products sold in the American Colonies. The colonists were required to buy stamps for these items—including playing cards and newspapers. They were furious!

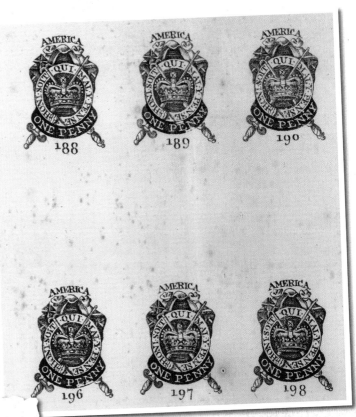

In late 1765 Parliament issued the Stamp Act. The act required colonists to purchase a stamp, such as the ones shown here, for all paper products, including newspapers.

A Colonial congress, called the Stamp Act Congress, assembled in New York to protest the Stamp Act. Representatives from nine of the 13 Colonies wrote the Declaration of Rights, which they sent to King George III and Parliament. Among other things, the colonists felt they shouldn't have to pay taxes unless they were allowed to participate in the government. They wanted to take part in the decisions that affected their everyday lives.

> *"... it is ... essential to the Freedom of a People, and the ... Right of Englishmen, that no Taxes be imposed on them, but with their own Consent, given personally, or by their Representatives."*
>
> —the third point of The Declaration of Rights of the Stamp Act Congress, 1765

The Declaration of Rights was sent to the king and Parliament to let them know that the colonists were not happy with the Stamp Act.

Tensions Rise

In New York and other colonies, leaders formed Committees of Correspondence to oppose the British taxes. The Committees of Correspondence helped the colonists spread important news and work together to fight Britain's actions in the American Colonies.

Men throughout the 13 Colonies also joined the Sons of Liberty. This group, which included lawyers, shopkeepers, and merchants, held meetings and led protests against the Stamp Act and other taxes. They also urged people to **boycott** British goods. They hoped their actions would force the king to put an end to the unfair taxes.

In 1766 the Stamp Act was **repealed**. But just a year later, the Townshend Acts were issued, placing taxes on glass, paint, lead, and tea. Fed up with the king and his taxes, the colonists began boycotting certain British goods.

The Townshend Acts were repealed in 1770, except for the tax on tea. At the time the American colonists consumed nearly 2 million pounds of tea per year.

Colonists in New York City expressed their anger toward the Stamp Act by holding protests.

In May 1773 Parliament passed the Tea Act. This act gave the British East India Company a monopoly on selling tea in the American Colonies. Parliament thought the colonists would be happy since the tea would be less expensive than Dutch tea **smuggled** into the colonies illegally. However, the British tea was still subject to the tax from the Townshend Acts. If the colonists accepted the British tea, they would be permitting themselves to be taxed without representation in the government. This only fueled the anger that the colonists were already feeling.

In New York City and Philadelphia, ships containing tea were sent back to England without unloading their cargo. But Boston's Sons of Liberty decided to have a "tea party." On December 16, 1773, they dumped 340 chests of tea (worth nearly $2 million in today's money) into Boston Harbor.

New York City's Tea Party

New York City had its own tea party, but on a much smaller scale than the one in Boston. When a ship arrived from England in April 1774, the captain said there was no tea on board. But the Sons of Liberty didn't believe him. When they inspected the ship, they found 18 chests of tea, which they threw overboard into the Hudson River. Later when the ship's captain sailed away, "The event was celebrated by the ringing of bells ... and a salute was fired."

King George III

The Continental Congress

The colonists realized that the problems with England were not going away. They began thinking about forming their own independent nation. In September 1774 the First Continental Congress met in Philadelphia. The group sent King George III the Declaration of Resolves—a list of complaints and the rights they felt they deserved. They also organized a formal boycott of all British goods in the American Colonies until the king addressed their complaints.

When King George refused to address the colonists' complaints, the Americans felt ignored and disrespected. They no longer wanted to compromise with the king. They wanted independence from Great Britain, and they were ready to go to war to get it.

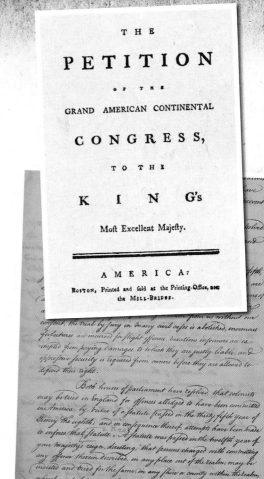

In the Declaration of Resolves, the colonists told the king that they wanted the full rights of British citizens.

> *"The die is now cast, the colonies must either submit or triumph. I do not wish to come to severer measures, but we must not retreat."*
>
> —King George's message to Prime Minister North following the Declaration of Resolves

smuggle—to bring something or someone into or out of a country secretly and often illegally

Chapter 7:
The Revolutionary War and Statehood

On April 19, 1775, the first battles of the Revolutionary War took place in Massachusetts. A year later the Continental Congress met again in Philadelphia. Four men from New York approved the Declaration of Independence on July 4, 1776.

The British Invasion

With the Revolutionary War in full swing, New York City served as the headquarters for the British military. By the end of 1776, thousands of British troops occupied New York City. **Patriots**, including George Washington and his troops, were forced to abandon the city. New York City remained under British control for the rest of the Revolutionary War. Many **Loyalists** made their homes there during the war.

Did You Know?

On July 9, 1776, the Declaration of Independence was read to the residents of New York City. Shortly after, a large crowd—including New York's Sons of Liberty—marched down the street to a nearby park. There they tore down a statue of King George III that weighed nearly two tons. Most of the lead from the statue was melted down to make musket balls, which the Continental army used during the Revolutionary War.

Fighting in New York

Almost one-third of the war's battles took place in New York. The two most famous battles in New York—collectively known as the Battle of Saratoga—occurred in September and October 1777.

In the two battles known collectively as the Battle of Saratoga, the British lost about twice as many men as the Americans.

A year and a half into the war, the Patriots were struggling against the larger, professionally trained British Army. On September 19, the first Battle of Saratoga took place at Freeman's Farm. Although the Americans retreated from the battlefield, they had fewer men wounded or killed. The Patriots' bravery on the battlefield forced the British to recognize them as worthy opponents for the first time.

The second Battle of Saratoga took place near a hill called Bemis Heights on October 7, 1777. Determined not to give up, the Patriots attacked the **Redcoats** from two sides. By the end of the day, as smoke filled the battlefield, British soldiers were dropping their guns and running to safety. During the night, the British abandoned their wounded troops and retreated up the Hudson River.

Patriot—one who sided with the colonies during the Revolutionary War
Loyalist—a colonist who was loyal to Great Britain during the Revolutionary War
Redcoats—a nickname for British soldiers, named after the color of their uniforms

But American General Horatio Gates and his troops followed the British. When they caught up with the Redcoats, they surrounded them until they had no choice but to surrender. The Battle of Saratoga was an important victory for the Americans and is considered a major turning point in the Revolutionary War.

The Tide Turns

The Patriot victory at Saratoga convinced the French to recognize American independence and enter the war against Great Britain. With the help of the French, the Continental army was able to defeat the massive British Army. After their defeat at the Battle of Yorktown, Virginia, in 1781, the British were forced to surrender. The Treaty of Paris was signed in September 1783, and the last British troops left New York City on November 25.

The Constitutional Convention

During the war the Continental Congress had created the Articles of Confederation, which set up the country's first national government. In September 1787 representatives meeting in Philadelphia signed the U.S. Constitution. It is still the basic framework for the U.S. government.

Alexander Hamilton (1755?–1804)

New Yorker Alexander Hamilton was an important founding father of the United States. Representing New York at the Constitutional Convention, he signed the U.S. Constitution in September 1787. Hamilton, fellow New Yorker John Jay, and James Madison wrote *The Federalist Papers*, which encouraged the colonies to **ratify** the Constitution.

From Colony to State

On July 26, 1788, New York became the 11th state when it ratified the U.S. Constitution. Albany became the state capital in 1797, and New York City served as the first capital of the United States until 1790. George Washington's first **inauguration** as president took place in New York City on April 30, 1789. New Yorkers filled the streets and celebrated.

New York grew rapidly after the Revolutionary War, with settlers coming from other states and countries. The population continued to be diverse, however New York maintained some of its unique Dutch character.

By 1800 New York City was the largest city in the United States and the trading and financial capital of the nation. These things are still true today, more than 200 years later.

George Washington takes the Oath of Office to become the first president of the United States.

New York City is now home to nearly 8.5 million people.

ratify—to formally approve a document
inauguration—a formal ceremony to swear a person into political office

Timeline

1524 Italian Giovanni da Verrazzano is likely the first European to see present-day New York while exploring for France.

1609 Henry Hudson is the first European to sail up the river named for him in New York.

1614 The Dutch East India Company builds Fort Nassau, a trading post in what is now Albany, New York.

1621 Dutch merchants organize the Dutch West India Company.

1624 The Dutch build Fort Orange on the Hudson River and establish the colony of New Netherland.

1625 Dutch settlers found New Amsterdam (present-day New York City) on Manhattan Island.

1626 Peter Minuit gives the Lenni Lenape tribe 60 guilders worth of goods in exchange for Manhattan Island.

1640 New Netherland Governor Willem Kieft goes to war with the Native Americans. More than 1,000 Native Americans are killed, and many Dutch farms are destroyed.

1647 Peter Stuyvesant becomes governor of New Netherland.

1664 Stuyvesant surrenders New Netherland to the English. The English rename the colony New York.

1673 The Dutch briefly recapture New York, but the English again have control a year later.

1683 New York's first General Assembly is elected.

1754 The French and Indian War wages until 1763. By winning the war, Great Britain gains Canada and most French territory east of the Mississippi River.

1764 Great Britain passes the Sugar Act to tax the colonists.

1765 Great Britain passes the Stamp Act, which is very unpopular in the American Colonies. The Stamp Act is repealed the following year.

1773 Colonists dump 340 chests of British tea into Boston Harbor.

1774 New Yorkers hold their own "tea party." The First Continental Congress meets in Philadelphia.

1775 The Revolutionary War begins on April 19 with battles in Massachusetts.

1776 The Declaration of Independence is approved on July 4.

1776 British troops take over New York City in September.

1777 The Patriots defeat the British at the Battle of Saratoga in October.

1781 On October 19 the British Army surrenders at Yorktown, Virginia, ending the major fighting of the Revolutionary War.

1783 The Treaty of Paris is signed on September 3, officially ending the Revolutionary War. Great Britain recognizes the United States as an independent nation. The British Army leaves New York City in November.

1787 Alexander Hamilton signs the U.S. Constitution representing New York. Hamilton, John Jay, and James Madison write *The Federalist Papers*, which encourages the states to ratify the Constitution.

1788 New York becomes the 11th state in the United States when it ratifies the U.S. Constitution on July 26.

1789 George Washington—the first president of the United States— is inaugurated in New York City on April 30.

Glossary

abolitionist (ab-uh-LI-shuhn-ist)—a person who worked to end slavery

ally (AL-eye)—a person or country that helps and supports another

borough (BUHR-oh)—one of the five divisions of New York City: Brooklyn, the Bronx, Manhattan, Queens, and Staten Island

boycott (BOY-kot)—to refuse to buy or use a product or service to protest something believed to be wrong or unfair

colonize (KAH-luh-nize)—to formally settle a new territory

generation (jen-uh-RAY-shuhn)—a group of people born around the same time

immigrant (IM-uh-gruhnt)—a person who moves from one country to live permanently in another

inauguration (in-aw-gyuh-RAY-shuhn)—a formal ceremony to swear a person into political office

Loyalist (LOI-uh-list)—a colonist who was loyal to Great Britain during the Revolutionary War

monopoly (muh-NOP-uh-lee)—a situation in which there is only one supplier of a good or service, and therefore that supplier can control the price

mutiny (MYOOT-uh-nee)—a revolt against the captain of a ship

natural resource (NACH-ur-uhl REE-sorss)—something in nature that people use, such as coal and trees

Parliament (PAR-luh-muhnt)—Great Britain's lawmaking body

Patriot (PAY-tree-uht)—one who sided with the colonies during the Revolutionary War

ratify (RAT-uh-fye)—to formally approve a document

Redcoats (RED-kohts)—a nickname for British soldiers, named after the color of their uniforms

repeal (ri-PEEL)—to officially cancel something, such as a law

shellfish (SHEL-FISH)—a sea animal protected by a shell; clams, oysters, and crabs are shellfish

silversmith (SIL-vur-smith)—a person who makes items out of silver

smallpox (SMAWL-poks)—a disease that spreads easily from person to person, causing chills, fever, and pimples that scar

smuggle (SMUHG-uhl)—to bring something or someone into or out of a country secretly and often illegally

Critical Thinking Using the Common Core

1. Compare and contrast women's rights in New Netherland with women's rights in the New York Colony. (Integration of Knowledge and Ideas)
2. Why didn't the residents of New Amsterdam put up a fight when the British invaded and took over in 1664? Use details from the text to support your answer. (Key Ideas and Details)
3. Why is the Battle of Saratoga considered a turning point in the Revolutionary War? (Key Ideas and Details)

Read More

Burgan, Michael. *The Untold Story of the Battle of Saratoga: A Turning Point in the Revolutionary War*. What You Didn't Know About the American Revolution. North Mankato, Minnesota: Compass Point Books, 2015.

Faust, Daniel R. *The Colony of New York*. New York: PowerKids Press, 2015.

Moss, Marissa. *America's Tea Parties: Not One but Four!* New York: Abrams Books for Young Readers, 2016.

Pratt, Mary K. *A Timeline History of the Thirteen Colonies*. Timeline Trackers: America's Beginnings. Minneapolis: Lerner Publications, 2014.

Schimel, Kate. *New York: The Dutch Colony of New Netherland*. New York: Rosen Classroom, 2012.

Internet Sites

FactHound offers a safe, fun way to find Internet sites related to this book. All of the sites on FactHound have been researched by our staff. Here's all you do:
Visit *www.facthound.com*
Type in this code: 9781515722342

Super-cool stuff! Check out projects, games and lots more at **www.capstonekids.com**

Source Notes

Page 13: callout quote: J. Franklin Jameson, ed. *Narratives of New Netherland, 1609–1664*. New York: Charles Scribner's Sons, 1909, p. 49. Accessed April 20, 2016. https://archive.org/stream/narrativesofnewn01jame#page/49/mode/2up.

Page 14: primary source box: "Peter Schagen Letter." *New Netherland Institute*. Accessed April 20, 2016. http://www.newnetherlandinstitute.org/history-and-heritage/additional-resources/dutch-treats/peter-schagen-letter/.

Page 21: primary source box: "The Surrender of New Netherland, 1664." *The Gilder Lehrman Institute of American History*. Accessed April 20, 2016. http://www.gilderlehrman.org/history-by-era/early-settlements/resources/surrender-new-netherland-1664.

Page 30, line 14: "The Atlantic World: America and the Netherlands." *Library of Congress and the National Library of the Netherlands*. Accessed April 20, 2016. http://memory.loc.gov/cgi-bin/ampage?collId=gckb&fileName=023/gckb023.db&recNum=2&itemLink=r?intldl/awkb:@field(DOCID+@lit(gckb023_0001))%230233&linkText=1.

Page 31: callout quote: Adolph B. Benson, ed. *The America of 1750: Peter Kalm's Travels in North America; The English Version of 1770*. New York: Dover Publications, 1966, p. 131.

Page 34, callout quote: "The Declaration of Rights of the Stamp Act Congress." *Constitution Society*. Accessed April 20, 2016. http://www.constitution.org/bcp/dor_sac.htm.

Page 36, sidebar, line 13: Albert Ulmann, "The Tea Party New York Had." *The New York Times*, January 21, 1899. Accessed April 20, 2016. http://query.nytimes.com/mem/archive-free/pdf?res=9A03E3DE1E39E433A25752C2A9679C94689ED7CF.

Page 37, callout quote: W. Bodham Donne, ed. *The correspondence of King George the Third with Lord North from 1768 to 1783*. London: John Murray, 1867, p. 202. Accessed April 20, 2016. https://archive.org/stream/correspondencek02georgoog#page/n300/mode/2up.

Select Bibliography

Benson, Adolph B., ed. *The America of 1750: Peter Kalm's Travels in North America; The English Version of 1770*. New York: Dover Publications, 1966.

Black, Jeremy. *George III: America's Last King*. New Haven, Conn.: Yale University Press, 2006.

Doherty, Craig A., and Katherine M. Doherty *New York*. New York: Facts on File, 2005.

Harris, Leslie M. *In the Shadow of Slavery: African Americans in New York City, 1626–1863*. Chicago: University of Chicago Press, 2003.

Jacobs, Jaap. *The Colony of New Netherland: A Dutch Settlement in Seventeenth-century America*. Ithaca, N.Y.: Cornell University Press, 2009.

Jameson, J. Franklin, ed. *Narratives of New Netherland, 1609–1664*. New York: Charles Scribner's Sons, 1909.

Kammen, Michael G. *Colonial New York: A History*. New York: Oxford University Press, 1996.

Lankevich, George J. *New York City: A Short History*. New York: New York University Press, 2002.

Taylor, Alan. *American Colonies*. New York: Viking, 2001.

Ulmann, Albert. "The Tea Party New York Had." *The New York Times*. January 21, 1899.

Willson, Beckles. *George III, as Man, Monarch and Statesman*. London: T. C. & E. C. Jack, 1907.

Regions of the 13 Colonies

Northern Colonies	Middle Colonies	Southern Colonies
Connecticut, Massachusetts, New Hampshire, Rhode Island	Delaware, New Jersey, New York, Pennsylvania	Georgia, Maryland, North Carolina, South Carolina, Virginia
land more suitable for hunting than farming; trees cut down for lumber; trapped wild animals for their meat and fur; fished in rivers, lakes, and ocean	the "Breadbasket" colonies—rich farmland, perfect for growing wheat, corn, rye, and other grains	soil better for growing tobacco, rice, and indigo; crops grown on huge farms called plantations; landowners depended heavily on servants and slaves to work in the fields

Index